The Essentia

Pia

SCOOTERS

All modern two-stroke & four-stroke automatic models
1991 to 2016

Your marque expert:
Henry Willis

VELOCE PUBLISHING
THE PUBLISHER OF FINE AUTOMOTIVE BOOKS

Essential Buyer's Guide Series
Alfa Romeo Alfasud
Alfa Romeo Giulia GT Coupé
Alfa Romeo Giulia Spider
Audi TT
Austin Seven
Austin-Healey Big Healeys
BMW E21 3 Series (1975-1983)
BMW E30 3 Series 1981 to 1994
BMW GS
BMW X5
BMW Z3 (1996-2002)
BSA 350, 441 & 500 Singles
BSA 500 & 650 Twins
BSA Bantam
Choosing, Using & Maintaining Your
Electric Bicycle
Citroën 2CV
Citroën ID & DS
Cobra Replicas
Corvette C2 Sting Ray 1963-1967
Ducati Bevel Twins
Ducati Desmodue Twins
Ducati Desmoquattro Twins – 851,
888, 916, 996, 998, ST4 1988 to
2004
Fiat 500 & 600
Ford Capri
Ford Escort Mk1 & Mk2
Ford Model T – All models 1909 to 1927
Ford Mustang - Fifth generation/S197
2005-2014
Ford RS Cosworth Sierra & Escort
Harley-Davidson Big Twins
Hinckley Triumph triples & fours 750,
900, 955, 1000, 1050, 1200
– 1991-2009
Honda CBR FireBlade
Honda CBR600 Hurricane
Honda SOHC Fours 1969-1984
Jaguar E-Type 3.8 & 4.2 litre
Jaguar E-type V12 5.3 litre

Jaguar Mark 1 & 2 (All models
including Daimler 2.5-litre V8) 1955
to 1969
Jaguar New XK 2005-2014
Jaguar S-Type – 1999 to 2007
Jaguar X-Type – 2001 to 2009
Jaguar XJ-S
Jaguar XJ6, XJ8 & XJR
Jaguar XK 120, 140 & 150
Jaguar XK8 & XKR (1996-2005)
Jaguar/Daimler XJ 1994-2003
Jaguar/Daimler XJ40
Jaguar/Daimler XJ6, XJ12 &
Sovereign
Kawasaki Z1 & Z900
Land Rover Series I, II & IIA
Land Rover Series III
Lotus Seven replicas & Caterham 7:
1973-2013
Mazda MX-5 Miata (Mk1 1989-97 &
Mk2 98-2001)
Mazda RX-8
Mercedes Benz Pagoda 230SL,
250SL & 280SL roadsters & coupés
Mercedes-Benz 190
Mercedes-Benz 280-560SL & SLC
Mercedes-Benz SL R129-series 1989
to 2001
Mercedes-Benz SLK
Mercedes-Benz W123
Mercedes-Benz W124 – All models
1984-1997
MG Midget & A-H Sprite
MG TD, TF & TF1500
MGA 1955-1962
MGB & MGB GT
MGF & MG TF
Mini
Morris Minor & 1000
Moto Guzzi 2-valve big twins
New Mini
Norton Commando

Peugeot 205 GTI
Piaggio Scooters – all modern
two-stroke & four-stroke automatic
models 1991 to 2016
Porsche 911 (964)
Porsche 911 (993)
Porsche 911 (996)
Porsche 911 (997) – First generation
model years 2004 to 2009
Porsche 911 (997) – Second
generation models 2009 to 2012
Porsche 911 Carrera 3.2
Porsche 911SC
Porsche 924 – All models 1976 to
1988
Porsche 928
Porsche 930 Turbo & 911 (930)
Turbo
Porsche 944
Porsche 986 Boxster
Porsche 987 Boxster & Cayman
Rolls-Royce Silver Shadow & Bentley
T-Series
Royal Enfield Bullet
Subaru Impreza
Sunbeam Alpine
Triumph 350 & 500 Twins
Triumph Bonneville
Triumph Herald & Vitesse
Triumph Spitfire & GT6
Triumph Stag
Triumph Thunderbird, Trophy & Tiger
Triumph TR6
Triumph TR7 & TR8
Velocette 350 & 500 Singles 1946
to 1970
Vespa Scooters – Classic 2-stroke
models 1960-2008
Volkswagen Bus
Volvo 700/900 Series
VW Beetle
VW Golf GTI

www.veloce.co.uk

For post publication news, updates and amendments relating to this book please scan the QR
code or visit www.veloce.co.uk/books/V4992

First published in November 2016 by Veloce Publishing Limited, Veloce House, Parkway Farm Business Park, Middle
Farm Way, Poundbury, Dorchester, Dorset, DT1 3AR, England.
Fax 01305 250479/e-mail info@veloce.co.uk/web www.veloce.co.uk or www.velocebooks.com.

ISBN: 978-1-845849-92-4 UPC: 6-36847-04992-8

Introduction
– what you can learn from this book

From the day Piaggio launched its first-ever motorcycle, the original Vespa, in an ambitious postwar Italy, the scooter has long been revered as an unconventional and modern take on the typical motorbike, evident in its underlying strand of style and fashion-conscious design. As trends have come and gone between then and the present day, the scooter remains a popular alternative to a motorcycle – yet its core values have changed once more, as automatic transmission machines now dominate the market.

For decades, Piaggio has been at the forefront of scooter product development, and so it is fitting that the iconic manufacturer operates today as one of Italy's leading automotive export brands. Piaggio bikes are in demand now more than ever before, and the manufacturer's expansive range of automatic two- and four-stroke scooters can be found in towns, cities and even rural hideaways across the globe. The world has embraced the modern scooter, moving away from the classic Vespa design of a two-stroke engine with manual gears, and now Piaggio's model range is key to the automatic scooter revolution.

Secondhand Piaggio scooters are plentiful on the used market, cost-effective to run, and still offer that exciting 'fun to ride' ingredient that has always been true for any scooter, classic or modern. There are more than 70 automatic used Piaggio and Vespa models to choose from, collectively delivering three key reasons to opt for a Piaggio scooter: affordability, practicality and versatility.

Buying a used bike represents the affordability element, especially compared to the purchase of a new scooter, while the subsequent financial investment required for a Piaggio bike's running costs is minimal. The great practicality of any scooter's day-to-day capabilities is undeniable, with many of these bikes the commuter hack of choice for urban dwellers, or even those further afield. The sheer number of models to choose from goes some way to explain how versatile the Piaggio scooter range is, while in day-to-day use, every bike is endlessly adaptable in its own right.

With so many used bikes out there, every scooter has lived its own life, so the buying process is not without its problems. This book will help reveal any issues in a given machine by equipping you with the knowledge and facts you'll need to to identify its true condition. Tips on spotting a dud versus a shining star in the classifieds sections are just the start of how these following pages will help shape your eventual purchase of a Piaggio scooter, whether it's a 50cc learner bike or a 500cc monster maxi scooter.

There's not only a variety of Piaggio and Vespa models to choose from, but colours, too.

This book is broken up into easy-to-understand sections that you can refer to along every step of the way; from selecting which model you'd like to set your sights on right through to going to view a bike and possibly riding it away. A helpful scoring system in Chapter 11 can be used to rate a scooter as you see it – this book is small enough to put in your pocket, so be sure to take this step-by-step guide with

Piaggio has fully embraced the maxi scooter revolution.

you for reference at any viewing.

In addition to buying advice, this book provides tips throughout on the experience of 'living with' a Piaggio scooter. From DIY mechanics to where to go for further help, this specialist information adds to a wealth of internet forum posts as technical advice becomes easier to access than ever before.

You'll never forget your first Piaggio bike, nor your second, third or even fourth. Italian scooters offer character and enjoyment like no other. Use this book to make

sure that this enjoyment is relished from day one: buy the right bike, and use the following information to treat it right. You'll be set for years of two-wheeled scooter fun.

All images in this book courtesy of Piaggio & C SpA unless otherwise stated.

The Vespa continues as a style icon, with the brand reborn under the guidance of Piaggio.

Contents

The Essential Buyer's Guide™ currency
At the time of publication a BG unit of currency "●" equals approximately
£1.00/US$1.32/Euro 1.20. Please adjust to suit current exchange rates.

1 Why an automatic Piaggio scooter?
– what are the main benefits?

Cheap to run

As well as being cheap to buy, Piaggio scooters are very economical to run. Typical fuel usage for a 125cc automatic scooter is 75-95 miles per gallon (mpg). Road tax (or the local equivalent) is very cheap for all scooters, especially the lower cc bikes. Servicing costs tend to be low, though this will depend on the age of the scooter and the power of the engine (two-stroke every 5000km; small four-stroke every 6000km; larger engines every 10,000km). Often cheaper than to run a motorbike, automatic scooters are immensely more economical than a car: fuel and running costs, tax and parking are a fraction of car costs for the solo rider.

Piaggio scooters are famously fun and easy to ride.

Easy to ride

No gear changes, and the 'twist and go' nature of automatic scooters makes riding one extremely easy to master. Unlike a motorbike, both brakes are on the handlebars, so the controls are very simple. Cornering and handling is spritely and fun. The majority of Piaggio bikes – those with smaller engines – can be ridden legally with only basic training. See Chapter 6 for more information on the kind of training/tests that you would need to undertake in order to ride your scooter on the road.

This modernvespa.com forum user demonstrates that it is straightforward to replace or upgrade parts. Even engine removal is simple. (Courtesy modernvespa.com)

Cheap parts

Most of the 50cc Piaggio scooters use the same engine, under different model names, and the same goes for the many 125cc models. As a result, parts are universally accessible for most bikes, should anything go wrong. The internet is awash with new and used parts – and an upshot for owners of older Piaggio bikes is that many bikes have come off the road to be broken up for cheap used spares. See Chapter 4 for more information on the cost of parts.

Easy DIY

Working on most Piaggio scooters is a breeze, even for the more inexperienced

DIY jobs on most Piaggio scooters are easy, and can be completed by have-a-go mechanics. (Author collection)

mechanic. A basic DIY service can be completed within an hour, and more complex jobs are generally straightforward for the enthusiastic home mechanic. Importantly, basic mechanical adjustments – such as brake cable settings, idle speed adjustments, or bulb replacement – can be made with relative ease. Clubs, user manuals and internet forums are a good way of getting advice for these kinds of jobs if you need it (see Chapter 15).

Reliability
The engine unit that many Piaggio models share is generally regarded as bullet-proof, with only an unlucky small percentage suffering internal parts failure. However, the bodywork can suffer from rust (see Minus points section on page 10). Treat your scooter correctly, with regular servicing and maintenance, and it will return the favour.

Selection of bikes
With a vast selection of at least 70 different Piaggio models to choose from, the classifieds are full of thousands of new and used bikes for sale at any given time. There's a bike out there to suit everyone, from small engine size to large; from city hack to motorway cruiser. Moreover, there's a bike to suit every pocket, too: see Chapters 3 and 4.

Small engine scooters, such as the 50cc Piaggio Zip, are ideal for learners.

The modern Vespa is a style icon of its day.

Style and appeal
There's no denying the 'cool' factor associated with a Vespa; yet the Piaggio brand has kudos of its own. Many prefer the charm of an Italian bike, as opposed to an alternative from Japan or elsewhere, and there are bikes in the Piaggio range intentionally designed to suit retro and sophisticated tastes.

For use throughout the year
A scooter is the perfect form of transport in a sweltering city on a hot day, but Piaggio scooters are as adept in near-freezing conditions as they are in the heat. Starter motors generally work in sub-zero temperatures, and the huge leg fairing can keep out the cold. Equally, a range of wind protector and leg cover accessories are available to keep you warm: see Chapter 4.

Hauling capacity
Modern scooters have excellent storage capacity. As well as the underseat storage, which should be large enough for your helmet, automatic scooters usually have useful compartments in the front fairing for phones, wallets and keys, etc. Some have a bag hook, while a rear pannier rack or top box may come with the bike or is worth investing in too.

Most bikes come with a bag hook to increase the amount you can carry while you ride.

Pillion passengers

Scooters with 125cc engines or above are powerful enough to carry a pillion passenger. Not recommended for 50cc bikes.

Town and country

With light and nimble handling, automatic Piaggio scooters are ideally suited for both country and town riding.

Piaggio scooters of most engine sizes will have sufficient power to carry pillions.

Many cities' motorcycle parking bays overflow due to demand. (Author collection)

Capture that Italian cosmopolitan chic with a Piaggio or Vespa scooter.

Vespa scooters are famed for their quirky colours, which add to the bikes' iconic design.

Minus points

Except for maxi scooters, Piaggios are not suitable for motorways or high speeds. Seats can be high on some models. Under-seat storage volume varies – will it be big enough for a helmet? Many models are susceptible to rust. Some auto owners miss the 'pop-pop' of a chugging two-stroke-engined scooter. Handling can be 'fun,' but you may miss the oomph that comes with a larger engine. Can be at the mercy of the elements – think about whether you will need to ride it throughout the winter months.

Alternatives

The Piaggio range is very comprehensive, but alternatives can be found: Peugeot, Suzuki and Yamaha are popular among twist-and-go scooter manufacturers, while Gilera and Italjet make small scooters. Chinese and Taiwanese bikes tend to be of lower quality, and other brands of imported scooters can be difficult to source and service.

The GP800 maxi scooter from Piaggio's sister brand, Gilera, is more powerful than any of the Piaggio scooter range.

2 Using a Piaggio scooter every day
– what's it like to live with one?

Many prospective scooter owners plan to use a Piaggio as an alternative to their regular car: for shorter journeys, regular commutes, or just nipping into town. Fit for any purpose, modern automatic scooters are versatile and dependable whatever the occasion.

While bikes with the smallest engine in the Piaggio scooter range – the 50cc scooters – are best left to learner riders, novices and for quick jaunts in the city, the rest of the Piaggio scooter range is adaptable and varied, but most of all easy to live with on a daily basis.

A 125cc engine – most common among all Piaggio bikes – gives you the freedom to use the bike for any journey you might want to make. Comfortable at cruising speeds of around 60mph, depending on load (rider, pillions and luggage), the 125cc engine falls short of being suitable for motorway speeds but is an ideal hack for town or country. These bikes can still easily complete multi-mile journeys avoiding motorways, while racking up miles by completing the same long commute on a daily basis will not faze any 125cc scooter.

Riders with the correct riding qualifications can move up the range of engine sizes. Added oomph makes for more comfortable riding, as acceleration is better, and the bike will sit happily at higher speeds, notably allowing for safe motorway riding, while that extra power generally helps in making the bike more usable as a daily hack.

If the idea of a larger engine is alluring, do bear in mind that running costs go up as a result: you'll use more fuel, insurance and tax are pricier, and servicing is more expensive. And while more power means faster speeds, also remember that this added weight of the engine and trim can make the largest scooters considerably heavier than you might expect, so this should definitely be a consideration when choosing a scooter.

Automatic transmission across the range makes for seamless ease of riding and by no means takes the fun out of the motorbike experience, as all scooters are nimble, fast around corners and quick off the line. The auto transmission makes a big difference if you'll clock up a lot of miles in the city – not having to worry about gears, as you would with a motorbike, changes the riding experience completely (most city riders say for the better).

Motorcycle parking bays of cities around the world have been transformed by the rise of the automatic scooter. (Author collection)

Piaggio scooters are generally reliable for daily use. As a rule, the older the scooter you buy, the more problems could come up, but the mechanical workings are simple so problems are easy to fix. You'd be unlucky to pick up any problems at all on a newer Piaggio scooter, though this depends on the quality of the short life the bike has led so far. This book will help you streamline this process and determine exactly what to look out for whether buying old or new.

Every Piaggio bike will be just as happy cruising in the city ...

If a Piaggio scooter will be your first taste of motorcycling – perhaps as a learner rider, or you're scaling down from a car – do bear the following in mind. Scooter riding exposes you to the elements, so think about whether you want to ride in all weathers (also if it's safe to do so). Chapter 4 has a list of suggested kit you'll need for the ride. Remember, you won't have a large car boot for shopping trips, so plan how you'll load up your bike before you set off. Also respect the limitations of a scooter, and weigh up the risks of each journey as it comes. Don't expect to be able to travel the same distances a car could, at the same speeds.

... as it will be out in the countryside.

3 Choosing the right bike
– which model is right for you?

The Piaggio model you choose will, of course, be based on your specific needs. There are currently just over 70 different Piaggio models on the roads, old and new, and this figure is increasing all the time as new models are released, or product line-ups are refined with different size engines, or new trim levels, and added to with special edition models.

The different types of Piaggio scooter available to buy can be split broadly into four groups: the Piaggio Vespa range; 'maxi' scooters; well-established older Piaggio scooters, and those scooters currently in production.

As a general rule, you should never buy a bike that is too powerful for your needs. Big-engine scooters are physically larger, so not only could the bike be too big for you, it'll cost more to run, and could even make you an unsafe rider. Instead, start at the bottom and work your way up. A 125cc scooter will suffice for most needs, and these are plentiful across each of the four sub-sections in the Piaggio model range.

Before we go into detail about the four categories, consider what you'll chiefly be using the bike for. Will it be for commuting great distances, or for short journeys across a few blocks in a city? Perhaps it'll be for something in-between. Whatever the purpose intended, this should be your main deciding factor.

Of the four categories in the Piaggio used model range, the maxi scooters are best for covering long commutes, and also provide increased comfort and the option of travelling at speed. They are, however, more expensive to run; not suitable for novice riders, and their large engines can be too complicated for DIY mechanics.

The Vespa range provides that added 'cool' factor, with styling consciously aimed at a trendy market. Under the skin of the Vespa bikes are Piaggio engines and parts; they also give much of the same riding experience as their plain Piaggio counterparts. Vespa scooters are great for day-to-day city riding, but can be relatively expensive to buy.

Older Piaggio models are cheap to buy and functional for everyday use. Newer scooters – used examples of those currently in production – give you the chance to buy 'nearly new' for added mod cons and the assurance of reliability.

Maxi range
Moving completely away from the template of a scooter as a step-through bike with

a small engine, maxi scooters have gained huge popularity since the introduction of the Piaggio BV200 in

Piaggio's maxi scooter range is especially popular in major European cities. (Author collection)

The 'B' or 'Beverly' range of Piaggio bikes is an entry point into the brand's range of maxi scooters.

2003. The market then evolved and Piaggio launched the 460cc X9 in 2005. Several maxi scooters have since been introduced to the range, adding power to the Piaggio line-up that is inclusive of certain models equipped with a 500cc engine.

These scooters are, to all intents and purposes, a conventional motorcycle with an automatic gearbox. Their large engines pack a power that dwarfs the rest of the Piaggio scooter range, and their wheels are much larger in circumference than those of other scooters. Especially popular in European cities, maxi scooters are the best of the Piaggio range for carrying pillion passengers, while it goes without saying that they're the most comfortable to ride, with armchair-like seats, in comparison to the relatively small seat foam found on the rest of the Piaggio range.

As much as a maxi scooter will give you extra clout and power on the road, it should not be forgotten that with the added size, weight and performance of a larger engine come the associated running costs. Not only will these maxi scooters cost more in fuel, they'll also set you back more to insure and tax; and, with engines bigger than conventional scooters, the size of the bikes is also considerably larger. If you're thinking about going down the 'maxi' route, make sure you have space at home to store one. Needless to say, these bikes are much heavier than normal, so are best left to a confident rider with the correct licence, training, and qualifications.

The B, BV or Beverley line of Piaggio's maxi scooters is available in 125cc, 200cc, 250cc, 300cc, 350cc or 500cc capacities. These bikes are smaller than the rest of the 'X' range.

The X scooters are popular with commuters and city dwellers alike. The

The Piaggio X-Evo's cockpit controls are more enclosed than usual; typical of the maxi scooter range.

Piaggio X7 is a mid-range maxi scooter, with engine sizes ranging from 125cc to 300cc. Moving through the numbers, the X8 is a similar mid-range bike with engine sizes from 125cc and up to 400cc. This model, now defunct, was replaced by the Piaggio X-Evo, a similar bike with the same range of engine choices, branded by the Italian company as a form of 'sporty commuting.' The X9 took things one step further with a choice of engine sizes featuring the most powerful yet, going from 125cc up to 500cc. The Piaggio X10 is most recent of them all, available with 350cc or 500cc engines.

Just as many of the maxi scooters enjoy the power that most conventional motorcycles would, these Piaggio bikes also benefit from the associated safety features. For example, the X10 comes with ABS braking on the 500cc model.

Compared to a conventional scooter, the X10 is a huge machine. With a choice of a 350cc or 500cc engine, it lives up to its maxi name.

Vespa range

This is a mainstay in the Piaggio model line-up since the introduction of the two- and four-stroke Vespa scooters in the 1990s. Since Vespa is a subsidiary brand of Piaggio, the bikes produced and released, either as Piaggios or as Piaggio Vespas, share many of the same blueprints, visual designs and parts. Of the 70+ bikes covered in this book, Vespa scooters make up more than half of all Piaggio models.

The capabilities of a modern Vespa are broad and varied, with a prospective scooter buyer spoilt for choice with the bikes available. The modern Vespa does away with its ancestors' characteristic two-stroke engine and geared transmission set-up by offering the market an easy-to-ride and versatile automatic city runaround.

At the lowest end of the price scale for buying a used Vespa, you can pick up a Piaggio Vespa ET2 or ET4 from around ●x300 now. ET4 scooters are most common with a 125cc engine, and while you'll notice that many in classifieds sections have had a hard life, these bikes can still be used as everyday transport despite many being nearly 20 years old.

The ET bikes underwent a facelift before being phased out in the mid-2000s, so the LX model of Piaggio Vespa became the accessible model for everyone, in 50cc, 125cc or 150cc

The ET4 is a great entry-level point into Vespa ownership. It's cheap to buy and there are plenty around. (Author collection)

The popular LX Vespa series inherits many features and style points once used on the ET bikes, as a scooter for the masses.

guise. Due to the number of LX bikes made, they're now cheap, plentiful and easy to buy on the used market. These small frame scooters were in production until 2014 when they made way for the introduction of the similarly sized Piaggio Vespa Primavera and Sprint scooters. The S model, in 50cc or 125cc form, is another small, recently made and readily available model.

For the rider looking for something that can pack the extra punch, the Piaggio Vespa GTS model range offers a little more than the average Vespa (not discounting the GT (Granturismo) and GTV models, made on a limited run as very similar bikes to the GTS). The GTS models have been designed with more than city riding in mind and so can be equipped for touring and long distance riding; notable accessory options include front luggage rails and a big rear pannier rack. Most importantly, the engine size of the GTS range goes up to 300cc, so these bikes can happily sit at motorway speeds and are generally more

Piaggio claims that the Primavera takes design cues from its namesake family predecessor from 1968, a classic two-stroke Vespa ...

... similarly, the Sprint can trace its name back to recurring model names in the Vespa family.

The GTS range of Vespa scooters is more aggressively styled. These bikes are suitable for light touring.

comfortable and capable than the rest of the Vespa range.

The stunning Vespa 946 is in a class of its own. With its single seat and delicately crafted curves, its design cues give the strongest nod yet to the acclaimed original Vespa range of the 1940s.

It's clear to see from where designers drew inspiration for the Vespa 946; notably with this Emporio Armani special edition.

The name of the new Vespa 946 makes direct reference to when the very first Vespa was launched in 1946 (pictured).

The 946 is available in a selection of appealing colour schemes.

Older Piaggio scooters

Just because Piaggio no longer makes a model doesn't mean you should discount it from your search. Older bikes are proven to have been successful and are plentiful in the classifieds sections. The likes of the Piaggio NRG, Sfera or Zip will evoke happy memories for those that were riding scooters in the 1990s.

The earliest models of Piaggio's automatic scooter revolution in the '90s, such as the Hexagon, Sfera and Skipper, typically had two-stroke engines and were most popular in 125cc form, with slightly smaller or larger displacement versions available at the time. The NRG, a 50cc scooter, has been the bike of choice for performance scooter enthusiasts, available on occasion with a rare, liquid-cooled engine. Various engine configurations were up for choice for suitors of the NRG, a bike that is elusive to this day, as tidy examples hold their values very well.

Bikes of the same era, such as the Carnaby, Diesis, Liberty, Storm and Typhoon, are hard to track down now, due to the fact that they were sold in low volumes upon release, and most have subsequently been scrapped. But many remain on the market today, the most accessible models left for secondhand purchases being the Fly, Liberty, Typhoon and Zip.

Generally speaking, many models are available with either 50cc or 125cc engines, giving you the choice of power output. Older Piaggio scooters from the mid-90s tend to come with a two-stroke engine, as do many 50cc scooters. But the majority of the range, especially those with a 125cc engine, are a four-stroke version making for smooth riding and great fuel efficiency.

The performance-orientated Piaggio NRG will revive happy memories for many, and it's still available to buy secondhand.

Currently in production

Excluding the aforementioned maxi scooters currently (and also excluding the three-wheeled Piaggio MP3, not covered in this book), the current Piaggio range includes the Liberty, Medley, New Fly, New Liberty, Typhoon and Zip.

With small wheels, lean styling and a punchy engine, the Typhoon stays true to conventional Piaggio scooter style.

Larger than normal wheels help this Medley model provide a more controlled ride.

The Piaggio Liberty follows a similar design path to that of its Medley sister model in both looks and functionality.

Small, yet fun, the Piaggio Zip is a great starter bike for anyone new to scooters or motorbikes.

Amongst this varied selection, buyers have a lot of different attributes to choose from based on their needs. The biggest choice a buyer will need to make is the engine size. Many of these bikes are available either as a 50cc or 125cc scooter (most 50cc bikes that Piaggio makes today do away with two-stroke technology, instead being made with a four-stroke engine).

As a point of interest, the new 125cc bikes adopt Piaggio's 3V (three-valve) engine, a new powertrain technology that the Italian company calls 'revolutionary.' With two intake and one exhaust valve, the engine uses electronic fuel-injection for 'class-leading' fuel efficiency and low emissions. If you are in the market for a new scooter, buying one of these could help keep the running costs down.

Of this current crop of Piaggio scooters, the Liberty, Medley and New Liberty get larger wheels for a smoother ride and better rider control – these bikes are also very fuel efficient and, often, they're the bike of choice for delivery firms and other businesses.

Just as has been the case with previous incarnations, all these later models retain the conventional scooter element in their looks and riding feel.

4 Considering purchase costs

– how much should you pay?

The right model of scooter for you will be determined by your needs for power and practicality, but the initial purchase price of a bike is also a key consideration.

Prices for Piaggio scooters are relatively low compared to conventional motorbikes. For the oldest bikes in the Piaggio range, tatty, used examples can be bought and run for next-to-nothing. The pricing scale gradually points upwards, however, generally set by a bike's youth and engine size, with the most powerful and newer scooters priced highest.

A one or two year old Piaggio scooter will likely cost close to the price of a brand new one, so sometimes it can make sense to buy new rather than used. This book largely gives advice for used bike purchases, but many of the points covered are be useful for buying new machines.

The Vespa range of Piaggio scooters tends to be most desirable, and such models hold their values well. The same can be said for maxi scooters, as long as they have been well cared for. Older Piaggio models – especially those made in the 1990s – tend to be among the cheapest to buy; notable examples include the Skipper, Typhoon, and Zip. These are plentiful within the classifieds, but you should take extra care when viewing high mileage or older scooters.

When buying used, you can expect some movement in price with a little friendly bartering. But don't turn up to a viewing expecting to chop lumps out of the seller's asking price. Using the guide outlined in Chapter 11, work your way through the viewing and understand what needs to be done on the bike. Then use these job costs as a bargaining chip – you'll have genuine reason to ask for money off. Don't go in asking for money off for no reason, though, as you'll probably just annoy the seller.

The following is a rough guide to used bike prices:

Vespa range
From end-of-life ET scooters to elusive models such as the GTS 300 ●x300-4000

Maxi range
Smaller 'B' or Beverly scooters are mid-sized maxi scooters, and so are cheapest. Newer models such as the X10 are of highest cost ●x1500-5000

Older Piaggio scooters
Bargains are available on older bikes, while many discontinued models are available in great condition for a fair price ●x200-2000

Currently in production
A lot of newer bikes are around on the used market already, but sometimes they're only slightly cheaper than brand new bikes ●x1500-4000.

Used Vespa models such as this GTS300 Touring are expensive to buy in the first place, but hold their value remarkably well.

Spare parts for Piaggio scooters are plentiful, and DIY mechanical tasks are easy. The following list will give you an idea of prices for common replacement parts. Note these prices are for used, reconditioned or pattern parts (most of these can be bought new and direct from Piaggio, but they cost at least three times as much, as a general guide).

Speedometer cable ●x15
Rear brake cable ●x15
Oil filter ●x3
Oil sump plug and washer ●x5
Air filter ●x7
Sparkplug (each) ●x5
Two litres of oil (enough for a service and a little left over for top-ups) ●x15
Front or rear brake pads ●x15
Front or rear tyres (excluding fitting) ●x40
Battery ●x30
Starter motor ●x20
Seat (inc locking mechanism) ●x80
Exhaust silencer ●x100
Body/frame of scooter ●x300
Used engine (inc transmission) ●x150

As well as protecting you from a crash, wearing the right gear will also keep you sheltered from the elements. The following is a guide for kitting yourself out with necessary clothing, with entry-level kit prices as follows:

Full-face helmet ●x150
Open-face helmet ●x75
Textile jacket ●x120
Leather jacket ●x200
Gloves ●x25
Boots ●x100
Protective jeans ●x75

Lastly, don't forget to price up those other essential accessories:

Weatherproof outdoor cover ●x50
Insurer-approved lock ●x60
Basic disc brake lock ●x15
Ground anchor (to lock to) ●x30
Basic portable tool kit ●x15
Top box ●x80

Slightly older models, such as the X9 maxi scooter, aren't made any more, so good used deals are available on the market. (Author collection)

5 Opening up the classifieds
– where's best to look?

Prospective buyers of Piaggio scooters are spoilt for choice when it comes to the big search. But one key question remains: do you buy privately or from a dealer? The pros and cons of each balance each other to the point it's like asking 'how long is a piece of string?'

The usual caveats of buying any used vehicle apply: buying from a dealer is generally more expensive, but you have the consumer security should anything go wrong; on the other hand, used deals will typically get you best value for money.

eBay
Ah, eBay, the everlasting pot of gold … yet also a likely tripping hazard if you're not careful. This is your best chance of bagging a bargain, yet also your most likely chance of buying a dud, so pay close attention to the buying tips throughout. From cheap projects to bikes from established dealerships, there's something for everyone on eBay (the site's main strength being the quantity of bikes on sale). The variation of buying formats – any number of classic auctions; 'Buy It Now' listings; and classified ads – expands on the choices available. A word of caution: never agree to buy a bike on eBay without going to look at it first!

Nation-specific websites
In the UK, the likes of *Auto Trader*, *Motorcycle News*' online listings, and *Car and Classic* are invaluable tools for scoping out used bikes, and can be used exclusively in a search. *Auto Trader* can turn up expensive bikes, but is high on quality. *Motorcycle News*' website features many scooters that aren't shown in the print edition of the publication's classifieds section, and is high in volume. *Car and Classic* pulls together classifieds from all over the web and is, by its very name, geared much more towards classic cars and motorbikes, but it's free to list. You'll find automatic Piaggio scooters on this site infrequently. *Gumtree* can be useful, but is untidy and tricky to use, especially as it lacks the spec-specific vehicle search tools that other websites offer. Take what all other websites have to offer with a pinch of salt. Further afield, websites such as *Leboncoin* have country-specific classifieds the world over.

Dealerships: new and used
Simply turning up at a scooter dealership and being led by a salesman can be a risky business. By and large, official and non-endorsed dealerships are trustworthy and can be a great place to buy a bike, but there is a chance that someone could try to offload you the dud that has been sitting on the forecourt for months. If you do pay an impromptu visit to a dealership, don't buy on impulse. Take heed of what's on offer, then go home and check similar spec bikes online. Are they the same price? Does it feel like you're getting a good deal?

Magazine classifieds
The days of popping down the shops to buy a motorbike magazine, to flick lustfully through the classifieds are largely behind us. Instead, most bike buyers do their research online, and use the web as a buying platform. Yet many established

magazines still have classifieds sections, which – though often free to use – are sparse in their listings. They're worth a look, and quite often you'll find bikes listed in here that are not advertised anywhere online. *Twist & Go* magazine sits alone as the only print publication dedicated to the automatic scooter in the UK. This features up-to-date price guides and classifieds. Aside from this, pay attention to the main motorcycle press, and also non-motorbike specific printed literature, such as local newspapers.

Imports

Bringing in a classic two-stroke Vespa from foreign shores might be commonplace, but doing likewise for modern, automatic Piaggio models is not worth the hassle. Most Piaggio models sold in Europe were sold simultaneously in the UK, removing the need to search foreign classifieds for rare models. Also consider the complication of converting a kph speedometer display to mph – and the mass of paperwork you'll have to fill out to register the bike. By all means, if you can pick up a bike for next-to-nothing, and you're already out that way with a van, it could just be cost effective. But it mostly won't be.

The internet has succeeded magazine and newspaper classifieds for bike ads, but printed listings are still worth checking out. (Author collection)

6 What are the running costs?
– factor these into your budget

Piaggio scooters are traditionally cheap to buy and, subsequently, to look after. This applies more so to the bikes with smaller engines, which tend to cost less to insure, tax and fuel, while their engines are easy to work on, helping to keep workshop labour costs down. It shouldn't be forgotten that once you've offered up the cash to buy a bike, there are several key cost considerations to make your vehicle road legal. These may even make you rethink the amount of money you want to spend on purchasing a bike, as they are a strict requirement and cannot be ignored.

Insurance
In most countries, you can't ride without insurance. The cost of this will depend upon you and your circumstances, but there are things that you can do to make it more cost effective. Selecting a Piaggio model with a smaller engine will help, as 50cc and 125cc bikes tend to return reasonable insurance quotes (as a guide, for a typical insurance premium in the UK, the average rider – with a 125cc automatic scooter, 25+ years old, living in a city – will pay just over ●x100 per annum). Third party insurance is cheaper, if available, but could leave you short in the event of an accident. Are you riding on a full motorcycle licence or on a provisional licence? The former makes for cheaper policies, as do advanced riding qualifications, and any no claims discount that you may have amassed on other bikes.

Road tax
Around the world, road tax is generally cheap for motorbikes, especially compared to cars. The rate for tax is often based on a bike's emissions – thus, engine size – so those with larger engines, emitting more gases, are taxed at a higher rate. Other countries and states around the world assess road tax based on a vehicle's weight, or by its market value. On a relative scale, whatever the criteria, a 50cc Piaggio Zip will be far cheaper to tax compared to a 500cc X9 maxi scooter, for example.

Servicing
The type of bike you buy will affect this – not just its style and engine size, but also its general condition. Has it been looked after by previous owners, and does it have a full service history? It you're not sure, you should have the bike serviced. At a reputable workshop, a full service will likely cost around ●x100 for most sizes of engine, accounting for most servicing tasks (changing oil, filters, sparkplug(s), investigating for faults). This 'full'

A small 50cc four-stroke bike such as the Fly can be ridden with really low running costs.

service should take place annually, so set aside a budget for this. While the bike is in for a service, ask the mechanic to check that the scooter will pass its next test of vehicle safety, roadworthiness and noise levels (MoT in the UK).

Workshop bills
Expect to have to pay to fix the odd thing here and there, especially on older bikes. Piaggio engines are largely regarded as bullet-proof, but some parts are prone to breaking. Speedo cables can snap, for example, light bulbs can fail, and batteries last only a couple of years. These are only suggested common problems, but bear in mind that, on older bikes, many plastic and light metal parts become brittle over time and can break easily. Have a plan in mind for what to do if something does go wrong, especially away from home. Factor in the cost for basic breakdown cover if ever you need to get the bike recovered.

Fuel
Owners of some 50cc Piaggio scooters will tell of a regular return of around 100mpg from a tank of fuel, which is cheap to fill in the first place, given the small tank size. Larger engines will comfortably give 50 to 100mpg, depending upon driving conditions. A 125cc Piaggio's fuel tank will hold around 10 litres, while the engine will return up to 180mpg, making for at least 150 miles of riding. Bigger bikes give less impressive figures, but are still economical. Budgeting for fuel won't be your biggest running cost consideration, but do take it into account.

Qualification to ride
A driving licence and your entitlement to ride a scooter are key, and how much you'll have to invest in this depends on where you'll be riding the scooter. In many European countries, you can jump on a 50cc scooter from the age of 14, with little or no training. Some countries across the globe require no formal training

Further riding training is always recommended. In the UK, you can sit a full motorbike test on an automatic scooter. (Courtesy ridesafe)

Further training will be requred in most countries before you can ride the 250cc Piaggio X9.

whatsoever. In most countries, though, you'll need to pay for formal training and qualifications before being able to ride.

In the UK, anything up to 125cc can be ridden on learner 'L' plates with a provisional licence and Compulsory Basic Training (CBT). Many other countries allow this easy access to scooter riding, without having to make you obtain a full bike licence. A full licence makes for cheaper insurance premiums, while you'll also gain extra skills as a rider, so you should be safer on the road as a result. In order to get hold of a full licence, you'll pay extra: for hours spent in training at a bike school; possible bike school motorcycle hire; and test fees. But you'll recoup these over time. Look out for advanced riding schemes to complement skills picked up in full licence training (UK examples include BikeSafe and the DVSA Enhanced Rider Scheme, as well as courses run by IAM or RoSPA).

Accessories

You've got your bike, it's road legal ... there's more to consider yet. Crucially, for starters, a helmet: open face lids are fine for city riding and are cheaper than full face options, those better suited for faster or rural riding. Safety protection gear should be considered, with a textile or leather motorcycle jacket recommended. If there's no shed or garage to keep the bike in, buy a cover. A lock should be used wherever you leave the bike: D-locks and chain locks are secure and can be stored under the bike's seat when not in use. Heated grips and bike sat-nav can be easily installed if required. Leg covers and fabric handlebar wind covers are popular among scooter riders in the winter months.

Leg covers are used by many in the winter as Piaggio scooters are ridden throughout the year.

The addition of a front screen takes the wind off your face: ideal for those who wish to ride with an open-face helmet ... (Courtesy twowheel.co.uk)

... which come in a variety of designs and styles. (Courtesy vespa.com)

Many riders fit handlebar muffs in addition to wearing gloves, while others question their safety. (Author collection)

Will you need a sat-nav for directions? Some Piaggio scooters are fitted with 12V power sockets for electrical accessories. (Courtesy TomTom)

7 Finding a perfect match
– which bikes to view and how to get it home if you buy

So, you've identified the model – or models – of Piaggio scooter you'd like to view. You've also established how much you can pay, and factored in running costs.

What is there still to do? Now begins the process of 'finding a perfect match' – one that you can realistically buy. Trawling the classifieds and finding the bike of your dreams at a bargain price on a remote Scottish island might appeal to the romanticist, but how realistic is it to even attempt going through with a purchase? In the same vein, setting your sights on a scooter far beyond your budget, with the faint hope of haggling the price down, is unwise.

Aim to narrow your search to around five bikes. These could be a mix of trade and private sales; if you're unsure exactly what model you want to buy, planning to view a variety of scooters is a good idea.

Location is key when scoping out potential bikes. Typically, you will find more choice in urban areas, so if you have the means to get a bike back home from your nearest big town or city, perhaps you could target your search there exclusively.

If using an online classifieds listing service – eBay, (or Auto Trader or Gumtree in the UK, for instance) – these allow you to search by geographical proximity. This is especially important on viewing a scooter, because you'll likely be restricted in how far you can ride it on the return leg home.

Ask the seller for the scooter's registration number, and run a HPI check (see Chapter 12) before you leave home. When you go to view, first check the documentation (see Chapter 12). Make sure it is all in order, before you go any further.

You might struggle to get an X-Evo into a van on your own, but the maxi scooters can be ridden for a greater distance. (Author collection)

If it's a private sale, ask the seller if they will be happy for you to take the bike for a test ride. Will their insurance cover you? Unlikely. If not, you will need to sort out your own insurance. If there is any chance you will buy the bike that day, you will need to have your own insurance to ride it home, unless you plan to take it home by trailer or alternative means. Generally, buying a bike on first sight is ill-advised. You should view a scooter, ride it, check various other points outlined in the book, and then go away, and take time to decide whether or not to buy it. But be prepared: you will need to bring a helmet and gloves for the test drive; if you do buy the bike, will you ride it home?

Alternatively, make plans to transport the bike in a van or trailer. This is a prerequisite for bikes that have been off the road for a long time, or are currently declared as off the road (this could be for any number of reasons: no current road safety test certificate, a mechanical fault, or otherwise). Piaggio scooters with relatively small engines are lightweight, so can be lifted into the back of a small van or onto a trailer by one person. Larger models are much heavier and will need two, unless you have a ramp. Make sure the bike is secured properly once in place.

Vehicle logistics companies often offer transnational movements of cars and motorbikes, but are expensive. However, the company will transport your bike securely and will be insured, which may be worth it for the peace of mind.

It may sound like a no-brainer, but make sure you have provision at home to store the scooter. Are you keeping it outside? Buy a decent all-weather cover. Are you keeping it in the garage? Make sure you have room for it, and that the space is secure. Do you need a permit to park a motorcycle on the road outside your house? Don't forget that for a bike to be kept on a public road in the UK it needs to be road legal, even if you won't ride it. This means that the bike is insured, taxed and has a valid MoT. Similar regulations are likely to apply in other countries.

Once you've chosen a bike to view, take a step back and imagine yourself owning it. Does it suit your style and your needs? Finally, choosing your bike should be a rational decision, but allowing your heart to have a say in proceedings can go a long way in securing long-term happiness and a bond with the bike.

Cover your scooter if it's going to be kept outside. (Courtesy vespa.com)

8 Items to take to an inspection

– these will help your viewing

So you've found a bike you'd like to view. Before you do so, consider arming yourself with the following to assist in the inspection process.

This book

This book has been written with the intention of helping you along every step of the way so do take it along to refer to when addressing specific points: Chapter 11 will be key here, as you can work through it while looking around a bike, and score where a scooter impresses or lets itself down.

Reading glasses (if needed)

If you need reading glasses to read text, make sure to bring them so you can consult this book. Likewise, you'll need to read documents and service history, as well as looking at parts of the bike up close.

A magnet

A small magnet can be used to detect that metal bodywork is consistent and without filler, which would indicate that the bike had likely undergone accident repair work. Do bear in mind that the scooter bodywork can be made up of large sections of plastic.

Screwdriver

Handy for poking around in nooks and crannies, examining the underside of the bike's chassis, within the inner workings of wheel hubs, and also in the engine bay. Use the screwdriver as gauge for rust patches by carefully and lightly tapping rusty bodywork to feel for the metal's strength. Get the owner's permission before you start poking around his/her bike and be sure not to scratch any part of the scooter.

Torch

While you're examining the inner workings of a bike, a torch is essential – even in daylight – for looking at seldom-seen inaccessible parts of an engine or underneath the scooter.

Voltmeter

For the technically minded, a voltmeter is useful for identifying existing electrical faults, if any. A simple check is to test that electricity flows consistently between battery terminals when all the bike's wires are hooked up. A voltmeter can also be used to test electrical parts in isolation, such as batteries, ignition components or lighting systems.

Overalls

Be prepared to get mucky: in order to look at all parts of the bike properly, you'll need

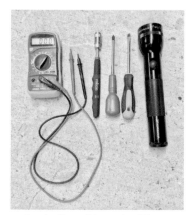

A selection of important items to take to a bike inspection: a voltmeter, magnet, screwdrivers, and a torch. (Author collection)

Don't forget your helmet and gloves
for that all-important test ride.
(Author collection)

to kneel down and/or lie on the floor. When you get into prodding around the engine, this will likely be oily.

Mirror on a stick
A mirror on a stick is useful for looking at other inaccessible bits of the bike – owing to the way Piaggio scooters are designed, these come in spades.

Digital camera/phone camera
Bring a camera along with the intention of taking a comprehensive selection of pictures that you can review later. This is especially useful when comparing several prospective purchases.

A friend
Do you know someone with a decent technical knowledge of motorbikes and scooters? They can offer an unbiased opinion to help keep your feet on the ground.

Helmet, gloves and riding equipment
Bring your helmet, gloves and other riding equipment should you end up buying on first sight – these are also essential for that all-important test ride.

Driving licence and other documents
Expect private and trade sellers to want to see licences, qualifications and insurance entitlement, before letting you loose on the road.

9 Fifteen minute evaluation

– looking around the bike

When you arrive to view a bike, take 15 minutes or so to assess the following basic points before you do anything else (certainly before you go out for a test ride on the bike). Reviewing your test ride is summed up in Chapter 11.

Exterior condition

How does the bike look, just standing there? Are there any evident dings, scrapes or parts of the bodywork that are obviously damaged? If so, ask yourself whether these will affect the running of the bike, while also bearing in mind that the bike could be structurally damaged as a result of these knocks. If there is damage to the bodywork, ask yourself whether you could live with a bike that is not cosmetically exemplary, and think about the money you'll lose selling the bike on.

Most Piaggio scooters are composed of a metal frame, and this will be a one-piece item of bodywork that makes up the front leg shields, floor boards, and also the bulk of the body towards the rear of the scooter that houses the engine. Many other parts of the bike will be made of plastic.

Think about how these different materials react to damage: in an accident, metal dents and plastic breaks. Use a fridge magnet to check if a panel is steel or plastic. Look over the bike while checking for dents in metal, and check that no plastic trim has snapped or broken off. Pay special attention to less visible areas that are still prone to damage, such as underneath the bike or behind mudguards.

Look at gaps where panels adjoin. Are there any peculiar gaps? The bodywork of every Piaggio scooter should flow smoothly without gaps between panels – quite often you can cross-reference this by looking at the other side of the bike, as most Piaggio models have a symmetrical design. If there are panel gaps, it means that panels have been removed (likely to fix something internally) and then not refitted correctly. Ask why the panels were off in the first place, what was fixed, and why the panels have not gone back on correctly. It could be that metal or plastic was broken when the panels were refitted, or that, at some point in the bike's life, someone has lost the bolts that secure the panels.

Pay special attention to rust – an eternal problem with older Piaggio scooters. It can crop up anywhere and with any strength of ferocity – it could just be a light patch that does not need urgent attention, or it could be eating away at an integral structural part of the frame, which is dangerous and is the most common cause of Piaggio scooters failing roadworthiness tests.

Bikes with rust patches larger than an inch in diameter on the bodywork should probably be avoided; as is the case with rust so aggressive that you could poke through these areas without much effort.

Scrapes here and there can be expected, but look carefully for rust that has developed as a result of chipped paintwork. (Author collection)

Running on idle

Ask the seller if you can start the bike. When you do, start it from cold. If you arrive at the viewing and the bike is warm (you can test this simply by holding your hand over the engine or exhaust silencer), ask the seller why it has been warmed up. They may be trying to cover up poor starting procedure from cold. When you start the bike, do so using the electic starter first, wait for the engine to find its idle speed, then turn it off with the key, checking for a smooth turning action of the ignition barrel at the same time.

Now start the bike again, but this time with the kickstart, if the bike has one. This is your opportunity to find out if both push button and kickstart procedures work. Don't expect any bike to start on the first push of the button or kick, but if the engine still doesn't fire after two or three attempts, this could point to a mechanical fault.

Leave the engine running for a while. It's important to know that the bike can maintain a steady idle without cutting out, running too fast/ slow, or spluttering. Listen carefully

If the bike has a kickstart, try it out.
This is an essential part of your check.
(Author collection)

for rough idling, and watch out for smoke. A little smoke on start-up is fine, but any more could spell problems. A tell-tale sign of a Piaggio scooter to avoid is one emitting blue smoke from the exhaust for an extended period of time. On checking the exhaust for excess smoke, follow the silencer pipe to the exhaust manifold, checking for leaks where metal pipes meet and are sealed by a gasket. Quite often, DIY mechanics remove exhaust silencers to access other parts of the bike, and then don't replace gaskets, causing leaks.

With the bike on its stand, leave the engine running for at least a couple of minutes and allow it to warm up – some Piaggio scooters come with an engine temperature gauge on the dash, either digital or analogue – otherwise, just feel the warmth of the engine with your hand without touching it. Revving the engine to the

Piaggio scooters like this Beverly have a temperature gauge. Check this works, and warm up the engine before riding.

point that the automatic gearbox wants to move the bike is good to test that the gearbox is sound, and that there are no knocking sounds from the engine upon acceleration.

Once warm, turn off the engine, leave it for a few seconds, then start it again on the electric start. Some bikes will appear fine after cold starting but have problems warm starting, so this check is essential. On a warm start, the bike should revert to its standard idle speed right away. Turn off the engine, and get ready to look at its mechanical parts in more detail before going for a test ride.

These checks should confirm an average or expected mechanical condition. If the bike fails any of these, concerns should be raised about its general operation, and you should be prepared to walk away.

Everything in place

Be prepared to get your hands dirty for this check. Begin by looking into all of the nooks and crannies around the bike. With the seller's permission, start poking around and examining everything you can see. Open up all of the compartments to make sure that the opening and locking mechanisms work: most Piaggio scooters should have under-seat storage, and a small compartment in the leg shield. Look out for extras, such as top boxes mounted on a pannier rack. Open them, shut them, lock them, and try it all once more to make sure nothing catches or is faulty.

You'll have had the engine running already for your review of the bike on idle. You don't need the bike running for this, but turn the key in the ignition to activate the bike's electronic working parts. Does the horn work? Check the brake lights, indicators, and headlamps (with some models you may need to start the engine for the latter to come on). While you check this, make sure that all sidelights, dipped and full beam are operational. Check that the fuel gauge works by watching where the needle moves to and comes to rest – if it sits at 'full' or 'empty' from the start and doesn't move again, it's probably broken. Try the various switches and buttons on the handlebars while you're looking at the bike's electrical condition.

This scooter has a glove box compartment in the leg shield fairing: these are prone to sticking on opening and closing. (Author collection)

Take the bike off its centre stand and put it on its sidestand, if it has one. How sturdy does it feel on each option? Put the bike back on its centre stand and use this as a pivot to get the front and then the rear wheels in the air, in order to examine them more closely. You may have to get a friend or the bike's owner to hold the bike while you do this. Both wheels should turn freely with the engine off, backward and forward. Expect a slight amount of brake rubbing on disc brakes, less on drum systems: these should turn freely.

Rotate the rear wheel forward – there should only be millimeters of lag before the transmission adds to the drag (you'll feel this kick in with your hand). Likewise, rock the wheels from side to side, checking for excess play in the wheel bearings. While you're looking at the wheels, ask a friend to grip the brake levers while the wheels are in the air. Check that the levers don't have excessive movement and that the brakes do their job by stopping the wheel from rotating. What are the tyres looking like? New tyres cost around ●x50 per wheel (including fitting), so take this into account when you come to value the bike.

Take the bike off its centre stand again and push it around in a short circle to check for odd noises – it's easier to listen out for these with the engine off. Any clunks or other odd noises should be investigated immediately.

Document checks

Only buy a scooter from an individual who can prove that they are the person named in the vehicle's registration document (V5C in the UK) and, preferably, at the address shown in the document. Also check that the VIN or frame and engine numbers of the motorcycle match the numbers in the registration document.

The seller should have all relevant documents in place and ready to look at upon your arrival. Don't accept missing paperwork or claims that they'll 'post them on if you buy the bike' or otherwise. The reality is that you'll never see these documents, if they exist at all.

Expect to see the bike's current roadworthiness test certificate (MoT or equivalent). Printed proof that the bike is, and has been, road taxed is a bonus, as it adds to the notion that the bike has been ridden legally by a sensible previous owner. If the bike was advertised with a full service history, expect to be shown a Piaggio service book with dealer stamps for every year since the bike was made. If the scooter was advertised with a partial service history, expect odd

How are the tyres looking on your bike? The intense black colour in this picture indicates that this tyre is nearly new.

service receipts here and there, but there is no set level of what can be classified as a partial service history. Has the bike ever been recorded as accident damaged? If so, checks of the relevant documentation are a must. If the bike has been imported, being able to trace this period in the scooter's history is important to understand with the help of a paper trail.

A log book (V5C, in the UK) is a prerequisite of any potential bike purchase. Bikes sold without these sometimes have a history of having been stolen or have been involved in accident damage, and not passing on this document is a way of hiding the facts. Applying for a new one in your name is also a lengthy process. Check that frame and engine numbers have not been tampered with. A frame number will often be on the bike's data plate, normally under the seat, while the engine number can typically be found on the outside of the engine's casing. If you carry out a HPI check before viewing, this often lists frame and/or engine numbers. Make a note of these and then compare them when you see the bike up close. If they don't match, question why and be prepared to walk away.

Anything else that the seller can offer for you to view, such as original instruction booklets or third-party maintenance manuals, are worth having.

Worth a closer look?

Getting the green light on all of the points mentioned above should be considered as essential for the purchase of any sound and reliable bike (choose which points you disregard if you're happy with a tatty runaround or a project bike). If the scooter falls short on too many of the checks listed in this chapter, perhaps it's best to walk away.

10 Key points
– where to look for problems

A varied range of paperwork – such as a log book, original booklet and service bills, seen here – is always a plus point. (Author collection)

Viewing the engine bay is a key check, but do you know what you're looking at? Ask an experienced friend to help if unsure. (Author collection)

Is there any obvious damage to either of the wheels, or the way they fix to the bike? (Author collection)

Check the bulbs all around the bike. Does everything light as it should at the front, back and sides?

Take a look at the exhaust silencer, checking for rust. Aftermarket exhaust systems should be avoided without prior research. (Courtesy modernscooters.co.uk)

11 Serious evaluation
– totting up the scores

This exercise will take around an hour and makes for a more detailed look at the bike you could be about to buy. To help you keep track of the bike's good or bad bits, use the scoring system throughout this chapter to judge just how this bike adds up, going from (4) as the best through to (1), the lowest mark. The scoring system is out of 100 points, and a breakdown of scoring categories is explained at the end to further assist in your decision-making process.

First impressions
Paintwork

Scrapes and knocks are an inevitable part of scooter riding, especially in the city. But you can still expect a used bike to have an acceptable standard of paintwork finish. Pay particular attention to parts of the bike that stick out, and so are prone to being caught on walls or edges. Wing mirrors and handlebar ends should get special treatment here. Likewise, think about if the bike was to fall over: where would it make contact with the ground? Then assess that point for damage, and if it has been covered up.

Bodywork

Take a step back from the bike. Look at its bodywork lines in general. Are there any obvious signs of accident damage (big dents or bits of the bike out of place)? Looking closer at the scooter, can you see any dings from small knocks? Look all around the bike, paying special attention to the metalwork (use the magnet in your inspection kit to test whether a part is metal or plastic), as this is most prone to dents. Large parts of most Piaggio scooters are plastic, so check for cracks and stress fractures. Is there any sign of body filler or accident repair work (again, use the magnet for this)?

Parts on the underside of the bike are prone to rust, like this centre stand. Make sure rust doesn't hamper its operation. (Author collection)

Panels, plastic and trim

Take a look at where separate panels on the bike join. Are there any panel gaps? No Piaggio model should have excess panel gaps. Where relevant, you can check to see if a gap is standard by looking at the other side of the bike, as it will have a symmetrical design. A lot of the time, adjoining panels will be plastic onto metal, and vice versa. Where panels join, has any plastic been snapped in refitting them? Look out for snapped plastic around the rest of the bike; also for missing bolts that hold on panels.

Rust

With all the salt and grit on the roads,

the underside of any bike is prone to rust more than any other part of the bike. Get on the ground and take a good look underneath the scooter, using a torch to peek into any nooks and crannies while getting a general feel for the frame's condition down below. Pay special attention to corners of the underside bodywork, where rust is most likely to begin before spreading into the centre of metal panels. Bolts and nuts can turn rusty, and then as a result cannot be undone. Look out for bolt heads/nuts that have already rounded off. Check engine ancillaries and adjoining parts of the chassis for rust or wear, such as the centre stand spring mechanism or other parts around the engine casing.

Leaks

A cracked sump could signal the end of an engine. Leaks from a weeping sump gasket are common, and while not ideal, they can be fixed. If you spot an oil leak, check the oil sump plug. If oil is coming from here, the leak should be treatable. From anywhere else, avoid the bike – it could have other weak gaskets or worse still, cracked engine casing. Most Piaggio scooter engines are air-cooled, so there won't be any coolant or water leaks. Look out for fuel leaks, though, as fuel pipes can easily get damaged. Fittings for fuel lines can also work themselves loose, and the rubber used will deteriorate over time. Stand the bike over a clean surface and watch for leaks while you're getting on with other checks, if possible.

Centre stand

Every bike will differ in terms of the stiffness in its centre stand. Some are a nightmare to use, some are so loose that you'll worry about the bike falling over. Make sure that this is just right. Of course, this is something that can be adjusted to suit your preference, but this can be a tricky thing to do. Take the bike off its centre stand, walk forward a couple of metres, put it back on again. Once back on the centre stand, does it feel secure and sturdy? Does the bike also come with a sidestand? Test this in a similar way.

Seat condition

How's it looking in general? If it's a colour, or even black, how true has it stayed to its original hue? Most seat covers are leather, so check that this is supple and not broken. Is it an original Piaggio seat? You should be able to check as it will have a Piaggio logo embossed in the print. Poke your finger into the seat body, made of foam, underneath the leather cover. Does this reveal soaked water? This will suggest the bike has been standing. Pay attention to the stitching and make sure the seat strap is still secured tightly (if fitted).

Under-seat storage

All Piaggio scooters should have helmet storage under the seat. An important check is to ensure that the plastic tray that sits under the seat is present. These are rare

This seat is old, but has retained its colour and stitching patterns. However, its strap is becoming loose. (Author collection)

Take a look to ensure that everything is present under the seat – including the main plastic helmet holder tray, battery cover, and fuel cap. (Author collection)

Under-seat storage is plentiful on the maxi scooters. Assess key operation, along with the space available.

and expensive to replace, even for the most common models. Also use this as an opportunity to judge the key operation when opening the under-seat storage area. Does the key stick? Or does it open smoothly?

All compartments open properly

Different bikes have various smaller cubby holes around the scooter that are often closeable so you can lock away small valuables such as phones, wallets, keys. Check that the glove holder compartment in the leg shield opens at the first attempt, and that it closes without difficulty, too. Ask the seller if there are any other cubby holes for storage, and test those.

Make sure all compartments around the bike open and close as they should.

Pannier racks/top boxes   4️⃣ 3️⃣ 2️⃣ 1️⃣

Many bikes will be fitted with a pannier rack as standard. Check that this is secured fast onto the bike – it should feel like it's part of the bodywork, and you'll be able to move the bike around by holding it. Flimsy pannier racks are dangerous and should be removed. If the bike comes with a top box, it scores extra points here.

Check how many keys come with the top box and assess its opening and closing action. Take it off the bike and attempt to refit it, this should be an easy thing to do.

A sturdy pannier rack is essential for the safe transit of items strapped onto it. (Author collection)

Tyres   4️⃣ 3️⃣ 2️⃣ 1️⃣

Take an initial look all around the tyres, looking at their shape. Are there any 'eggs,' bumps or lacerations? Then look at them in more detail. Is the rubber visibly aged – with a faded black shade and cracks in the tyres – or do they look newer? Can you tell how much life the tyres have left in them? Try and gauge how much tread is left. In the UK, the minimum limit for bikes over 50cc is 1mm of tread across ¾ of the width of the tyre and visible tread on the remaining ¼. Scooters up to 50cc must be fitted with tyres that display the grooves of the original tread pattern and it has to be clearly visible. Also check for uneven wear, as this could spell problems with the way the bike rides. Poke around the tyres and make sure they're hard and thus inflated; if pressures are very low it suggests that the bike has been ridden on under-inflated tyres for a while, so they should be renewed. DOT numbers on sidewalls tell us when tyres were made, identified thus: An example of 'DOT EB V3 BRD 2215' will tell us that a tyre was made in the 22nd calendar week of 2015. The '22' in the last four digits of the DOT number is the week, the '15' is the year; this is an adaptable and widely used format for identifying age. If the tyre is over five years old, it'll need replacing.

If the bike comes with a top box, does it open and shut correctly? How many keys come with it? (Author collection)

Free play in the wheels   4️⃣ 3️⃣ 2️⃣ 1️⃣

While you're checking the tyres, assess how the front and rear wheels look and feel. With the bike on the centre stand, get a friend to hold down the rear of the bike so the front wheel is in the air. Roll it around, checking for smooth running, and then, in a vertical plane, rock it from side to side – any play indicates worn wheel bearings. Repeat for the rear wheel, but also turn the wheel backward and forward, checking to see how soon the transmission kicks in – you'll feel this as a light pull that adds to the wheel's turning resistance – it should kick in within one tenth of a turn of the wheel.

Free play in headset bearings

Push the back of the bike down so it pivots on its centre stand, and the front wheel is suspended in the air (you may need to get your friend to do this while you carry out the check). Turn the handlebars full lock from left to right, while the front wheel is in the air. The bars should turn freely, with no sticking points at all. If they do catch, it probably means that the headset bearings are corroded, or that they are beginning to corrode. It could also mean that cables

You don't need to go this far to check smooth operation of headset bearings. (Author collection)

or parts of bodywork panels are getting in the way of the handlebars.

Electrics

Battery

The battery is located under the seat, under a plastic lid and is accessible by removing a screw or bolt. Simply looking at the battery should give you a clue as to its condition – how old is it compared to the age of the bike? Is it an original from Piaggio? Does it look old and scruffy? A good battery is crucial for the efficient starting procedure of a bike. If you're able to bring a voltmeter to the inspection, use this on the battery to test that its output is standard and consistent. Measure the voltage with the engine both off and running. All Piaggio scooters have a 12v electrical system.

A typical scooter battery in good condition. (Author collection)

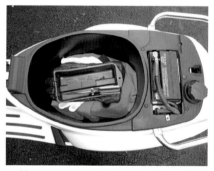

More often than not, the battery will be located under the seat on a Piaggio scooter. (Author collection)

Lights

Working around the bike, check that all lights work. You may need to start the engine to get the sidelights, dipped and full beam to work on some models. On other models you should be able to test indicators and brake lights with the ignition on but without the engine running. Bulbs can appear dim when the engine is revving at a low speed and they will become much brighter on revving the engine. This is

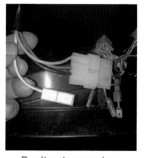

Make a full check on all light functions around the bike, not just at the front.

Don't get your wires crossed: electrical problems on older Piaggio bikes are a common issue. (Author collection)

normal – don't think that this is a fault in the electrical system. Make sure that the transition between dipped and full beam is seamless, and with no delay.

Handlebar instruments and dials

Look at the handlebar instrument panel. Take a moment to understand what every switch and button does: the start button, the engine kill switch, light switches, indicator switches, the horn, others. In turn, try each of these out, and then check to see that their action works correctly – ie when you indicate right, do all indicator bulbs on the right side of the bike work? Do the indicators then cancel with a push of the switch?

When you turn on the ignition, does the dashboard instrument panel appear to be working? Make sure no display bulbs are faulty.

Take a moment to familiarise yourself with the switches on the handlebars before trying out all of them.

Throttle

Here, you're checking for it sticking during operation – make sure that the throttle can open and return freely to the shut position. **Caution! Do not** make this test with the engine running (or the bike will shoot off on its own down the road!)

Fuel gauge

Turn the ignition key to the ignition on position. The fuel gauge should show a fuel level without the engine running. Does it look accurate? If you can, peer into the fuel tank and try to determine whether the gauge is telling the truth or not. Many Piaggio scooters' fuel tanks are curved and shaped so you can't see into them. If the gauge reads 'empty' or 'full' straight away and doesn't move, this can signal a false reading.

Engine
Appearance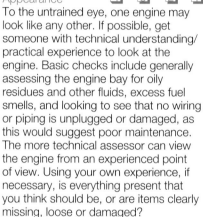

To the untrained eye, one engine may look like any other. If possible, get someone with technical understanding/ practical experience to look at the engine. Basic checks include generally assessing the engine bay for oily residues and other fluids, excess fuel smells, and looking to see that no wiring or piping is unplugged or damaged, as this would suggest poor maintenance. The more technical assessor can view the engine from an experienced point of view. Using your own experience, if necessary, is everything present that you think should be, or are items clearly missing, loose or damaged?

Check oil

A basic check that can expose nasty surprises in the first instance. Amazingly, a lot of Piaggio scooters are run without sufficient oil (by careless owners or those with disregard for basic maintenance). Older bikes especially are known for burning oil, so the oil level must be checked on a regular basis and topped-up when necessary. Older Piaggio engines will have an engine window sight glass to view oil levels, while newer bikes will have a manual dipstick to check and, likely, oil level gauges in the instrument panel. When looking at the oil, a golden colour is preferred to black, or strongly discoloured oil.

Check the fuel gauge. If it works, you're in luck, but never rely on it. These are famously inaccurate and temperamental. (Author collection)

The inner workings of a Piaggio scooter's transmission. Don't worry, this is not part of the inspection! (Author collection)

Check the oil. On this scooter, the oil level can be seen through a sight glass. More modern models will have a dipstick. (Author collection)

Start-up

Time to fire up the engine. You'll have checked this in Chapter 9; now it's time to rate its performance with a score. Begin by starting the bike with the electronic push-button start. If it fires up straight away, then full marks. If it's hesitant, and turns over a few times before firing, this can be normal; any longer and it's a cause for concern. Likewise, try with the kickstart, if the bike has one. Don't expect the bike to start on the first kick, but it should go on the second or third. Watch out for a slipping kickstart lever, as this suggests internal linkage mechanisms are out of alignment.

Smoke and excess noise

Some exhaust systems are noisier than they should be, sometimes by intentional modification. If noisy, the bike's exhaust silencer may have been refitted without a new gasket. While holding the back brake and with the engine running, twist the accelerator to increase the revs, and make sure that the exhaust noise doesn't get substantially worse as the engine works harder. Listen to the the the exhaust's tone: it should be clear if something is wrong. Also observe the exhaust smoking as the engine runs. Expect a little smoke on start-up, but it shouldn't continue after a few seconds.

The exhaust system here is factory standard and looks like new, so shouldn't cause any problems. (Author collection)

Brakes – levers

How do the brake levers feel when you pull them? They should feel prompt without being too sharp or grabby. At the other end of the scale, ensure that the brake levers don't feel loose or sticky – especially on a cable brake set-up. When you pull a brake lever, it should stop parallel with the handlebars and travel no further. An accurate return action on the brake levers is essential. Check that no parts of the lever are missing – eg the circular end part that helps fingers grip the levers.

Exhaust silencer – rust

One of the worst areas for rust on Piaggio scooters is typically the exhaust silencer. Particularly on older scooters, these silencers can rust to the point that they look like they've been excavated from the deep sea. This can result in the exhaust blowing, and general poor performance. It also lets down the look of the bike cosmetically. Check for holes on a rusty exhaust, especially at gasket joining points, right up to the exhaust manifold on the engine if it is in view. Look to replace a rusty exhaust if you buy the bike.

This rusty exhaust silencer has seen better days, and will need replacing soon. (Author collection)

The test ride

This part of the check process is strongly recommended, but only if possible. Importantly, you need the consent of the seller to ride the bike, before you're let loose on the road with their scooter. Understandably, some sellers won't allow test rides at all, but do your best to gain this opportunity that allows you to get a true feel for how the bike really stacks up. After all, it will be you riding the machine, if you buy it.

Hopefully you'll have remembered your helmet and gloves – and also your driving licence, insurance documentation and anything else that can help you prove to the seller that you're correctly qualified to ride. If you have existing bike insurance, check the level of cover you're entitled to for riding other people's bikes. If you can only offer the seller third-party insurance for the test ride, you'll have to give your word that you'll pay for anything you damage. Some sellers may also insist that you leave something of equivalent worth with them, so you don't ride away with the bike. Perhaps the friend you bring could be your bargaining chip.

Your first ride will be one to remember, but don't get distracted, and remember to be critical, while at the same time enjoying the occasion.

If you're not familiar with the area, ask the seller if they can suggest a 15 minute loop; this should allow you ample time for a qualified assessment.

With the engine running and the bike stood still, listen out carefully for odd noises, rattles and spluttering. Apply the back brake, and twist the throttle to make the engine work through its rev range at a standstill. Malicious clinks and clunks could come from anywhere on the bike, so lend an ear all around the scooter – from around the engine bay to the exhaust. If you do hear anything odd, try to identify what it is and what's causing it. Once an engine has warmed up and is on idle, you should experience smooth running with no rough or undulating rev patterns.

Set off. Does the speedometer work, and does it feel accurate based on the speeds it claims you are travelling? Are the units of the speedometer correct for the country in which you're buying the bike (mph or kph)? If you have a chance, make a note of the mileage at the start of your test ride, then measure this against the finish point. This will determine whether the odometer works. If it is stuck or fixed, it would show a false reading.

On setting off, take note of how responsive the bike feels to acceleration. Is it laggy or slow – or does it feel smooth and reactive? Get up to speed, and sit with the flow of the traffic on the road, simulating real-world riding conditions. Try to build in a mixture of roads into your route, allowing you to experience the bike at

Looking at the suspension springs and other components, is there any obvious sign of wear or rust? (Author collection)

Check the speedometer and instrument panel area for any faults.

Looking at the brake levers, are they intact without chips or scrapes? When you operate them, do they feel too tight or loose? (Author collection)

How did the brakes feel out on the test ride? Make sure you're comfortable with their stopping power.

an assortment of speeds. Relax in your riding position and feel for excess vibration coming through your hands and arms from the handlebars, both at standstill and when moving.

Experienced riders can assess how the bike corners with light leaning exercises, making sure that the bike feels settled when being leant around a bend.

How does the bike feel as it works its way up to speed? Most Piaggio scooters' automatic transmission systems will be made up of a small number of gears – the rider has no control over their selection – but it's important that the bike is comfortable going from slow to fast, and then back again. Make note of how this feels in both acceleration and deceleration. Any delay or odd behaviour with the gearbox could spell a deep-rooted problem, and transmission problems can be costly to fix.

Do the brakes feel like they're correctly set up? Bear in mind that if your bike is fitted with drum brakes, they may not be as responsive as disc brakes. Many

Piaggio scooters will have a disc brake on the front – as the power brake – and a drum brake on the rear. On your test ride, you should try the brakes at various speeds, making sure that they do not lock, and are responsive and predictable in all situations (always check for traffic around you before doing so). Models equipped with ABS can be assessed based on this – the braking action should be accurate and effective from high speeds.

You really shouldn't notice the suspension working, but it'll be clear that something is wrong if the bike feels notchy going over bumps, or if you can hear the suspension mechanisms working. If handling feels spongy and lethargic excess play in the suspension bushes or worn shock absorbers are likely culprits. Piaggio scooters generally give a comfortable ride, so the suspension shouldn't be feel too firm.

After your test ride, the engine should be running at its optimum temperature. Turn off the bike, wait a few seconds, and try starting it again, first with the electronic push starter, and then with the kickstart (if the bike has one). This check will eliminate the possibility of any warm starting issues, which are a direct nod to fuel/air mixture problems. The bike should return to its set idle speed straight after starting when warm.

Evaluation procedure
How does the bike score?

90 to 100 = Perfection. As long as you can agree on a price, don't miss this bike.
80 to 89 = Pretty much there. It's very good, and while one or two things let it down, you have something to bargain on.
70 to 79 = Average to good. You may need to spend money straight away.
60 to 69 = Below average: careful consideration required.
50 to 59 = Only consider this if the money is right. It'll be expensive to improve.
40 to 49 = Poor. Perhaps a project bike, or a very cheap runaround.
Below 39 = Walk away or you may you spend more money fixing the bike than you paid for it.

12 Paperwork matters
– does the bike's history stack up?

The paper trail
A wallet full of paperwork can tell you a lot about a bike, and may be the deciding factor in whether you buy or walk away. Careful collection of paperwork generally means a bike has been looked after by its owner(s). Missing documents could suggest a general lack of attentiveness. If paperwork is missing, there could even be a serious problem lurking. Furthermore, if you have all the paperwork, it will make the bike easier to sell; without, it might be harder to sell or you'll sell for less.

Log book
In the UK, a vehicle's log book (V5C) document is vital. Other countries will have an equivalent, often referred to as a vehicle registration certificate or a 'pink slip.' It tells us where and to whom a vehicle is registered, the vehicle's registration number and more. Is it genuine? Genuine documents have a watermark. If there is no registration document, or if it is not registered to the person selling it, walk away.

Service history
Piaggio scooters will have left the showroom with a service booklet, setting out a suggested service schedule (based on miles covered or time passed). A full service history is an asset to any bike and adds value. Absence of servicing records can work in your favour when bargaining, but take into account that you may have to pay for servicing in the near future. Look out for bonus receipts for ad-hoc jobs done professionally. Bear in mind that some Piaggio owners with basic mechanical skills carry out servicing and repair work themselves, for which obtaining receipts can be tricky. If the owner has carried out work, they may have photographs. Ask if they will let you have copies.

Road safety test certificates
If you buy a bike with a valid road safety certificate (MoT in the UK), make sure the owner gives it to you. This document does more than prove a bike's roadworthiness. Old certificates are a reliable way of verifying genuine mileage, as this is noted at every MoT in the UK. With this you can tell if the bike has been standing or has covered an unreasonable amount of miles in one short period – or even worse, if the bike has been clocked. Replacing lost certificates can be difficult so be wary of this. It's also possible to check MoT history on the UK government's website.

VIN
Not a document that the seller can produce, but an important piece of the bike's paperwork trail that you need to check. Ideally, you should try and find out the bike's VIN (Vehicle Identification Number) before you view the scooter, this can be obtained via an HPI check (see below). Then, as soon as you view the bike, check that the VIN matches the reference stored in official records – if it doesn't, walk away. The VIN is typically on a Piaggio's data plate, installed under the seat of most bikes (you may have to remove the plastic tray to find it). Make sure that the embossed VIN has not been scratched out, painted over or otherwise tampered with.

HPI checks

An HPI check, in the UK, reveals the full history of a vehicle, based on its numberplate, and will include some or all of the following: whether it has been recorded as stolen, an insurance write-off, or scrapped; number of previous owners; mileage discrepancies; numberplate change; outstanding finance on the vehicle; the VIN number; and a valuation. For a motorbike or scooter, an online check can cost as little as ●x5 (●x20 for the most comprehensive). Other countries have similar vehicle history report schemes, that scour the same information fields to protect consumers from buying unsafe vehicles. In the US, for example, a multitude of third party websites can check a VIN reference for upwards of ●x5.

Insurance write-offs

In the UK, Category C or D repairs apply to vehicles that have been involved in an accident previously, but have been repaired satisfactorily. There's nothing wrong with knowingly buying a bike that has been written-off for accident damage before, though only under certain conditions. Clearly, the repair work should be of an acceptable standard. It should be obvious where you need to look after asking the seller about the repairs. Documents are equally key: communications from the insurance company are useful, as you have a rundown of events in writing. A vehicle's Category C or D status is marked on the log book document. Category C and D vehicles can be harder to sell on. If you decide to buy, make sure the price you pay reflects this.

Restoration documentation

Newer Piaggio models are too recent to have been restored, but bikes made throughout the 1990s are increasingly a target for full restoration, as owners patch up rusty framework, while also stripping and rebuilding engines. While bearing in mind that much of the bike won't be original – and so receipts for new parts should be provided – ask for pictures and details of the restoration process. Did the restorer do the work on a shoestring budget? Have they used the correct parts? What was wrong with the bike in the first place? Also make sure VINs still match and that they haven't been painted or scratched out.

Official literature

You'd be surprised by how helpful original instruction manuals and handbooks can be for Piaggio scooters of all ages. It's useful to have these for quick reference, whether for reading up on your model's unique history or checking to find a recommended engine oil. Official Piaggio and Vespa posters and sales brochures specific to the bike's model help it retain its value should you ever sell it on.

13 Weighing up the work
– are you prepared to take on a project?

This section mostly applies to older Piaggio models made throughout the 1990s and 2000s. Many bikes made in this time period have either lived a life outside, inviting rust, or have covered a huge amount of miles. But let's not forget, munching up the miles is what Piaggio scooters are good at doing. With a little bit of TLC and financial investment, you can turn a tatty project into a bike to use every day, but it needs an educated assessment before making the commitment to buy.

Piaggio scooters are very easy to work on, should you be inclined to take on the work yourself, and the wealth of secondhand parts on eBay ranges from rare small screws to complete engines. See Chapter 4 for a list of guide prices of common spare parts. Most mechanical parts can be fitted to a variety of Piaggio models, owing to the fact that many bikes use the same engine. Some bike shops and Piaggio specialist workshops do take on project bikes for a likely fixed fee – just make sure you do your research and agree on a price before striking a deal, to avoid nasty hidden surprises. Also take into account the extra money you'll have to spend getting a non-runner bike to a garage in a van or on the back of a trailer.

Purchase prices for project bikes will, of course, be cheaper than those that are already roadworthy. This may often only be a difference of around ●x200, so it's always worth weighing up whether a project is worth taking on at all, as you might spend more getting it road ready than if you were to simply buy a complete bike.

Also consider how successful you might be trying to sell on a completed project (or worse still, an unfinished bike in bits) compared to a scoot that's not been tampered

If you're looking into buying an older scooter, it could be worth considering buying a second bike, for a constant supply of spares. (Author collection)

You never know what's lurking in the next parking bay ... (Author collection)

Don't be afraid to take on drastic mechanical work. Complete engine swaps are achievable for intermediate-level mechanics. (Author collection)

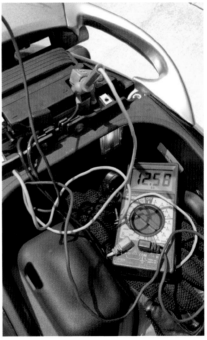

Unfortunately, this accident-damaged bike is beyond repair: a negative aspect of using irreparable plastics in the bodywork of some Piaggio bikes. (Author collection)

You might be reluctant to bring out the voltmeter, but it is advisable for older bikes, as electrical problems do occur. (Author collection)

with. Buyers will always prefer an accountable, linear life of a bike because the mechanical reliability of one that has been restored is just so uncertain.

When you come to take on the work, it's worth spending a little extra money on a handful of reputable books that will assist in your project revival process: workshop manuals specific to your model of bike, general motorcycle restoration guides, and general mechanical reference work books are useful. Internet forums can also be handy for following others' build stories of other projects; this will give you an idea of what to expect. Forums can also be used to diagnose ongoing mechanical faults, but always back up these findings with your own mechanical understanding (see Chapter 15 for a selection of recommended helpful Piaggio forums).

Some project bikes in the classifieds will be insurance write-offs. Approach these with caution, yet by no means should they be avoided completely. Some may have been written-off for small scrapes, yet some could have more deep-rooted damage – make sure to do your homework. Insurance write-off bikes typically require replacing of panels and the fairing, which are much harder to find than mechanical parts, and can be expensive. Take this into account, and bear in mind you may not be able to replace cracked, bent or misshaped fairing at all.

Questions and answers
These are aimed at those prepared to take the restoration work into their own hands, because the success of any project will hinge upon the time you invest in it, and also your mechanical skills. An affirmative nod to most of these, and it's game on:
- Do you understand the basic mechanical running of a two- or four-stroke engine?
- Are you confident with basic electrical systems maintenance, and can you use a voltmeter?
- Do you have a basic set of metric socket tools, as well as other toolbox essentials, such as large and small screwdrivers, pliers, etc?
- Moreover, do you own heavier tools? Namely, a crowbar, torque wrench, mallet, hammer, drill, large wrench and workbench with vice?
- Do you own inspection equipment, such as an inspection mirror and gauge sets?
- Do you have tools to extract or fix rusty, damaged or snapped bolts? Can you tap new threads? Have you dealt with rounded-off bolt heads before?
- Have you ever welded? You may need to do so for rusty frame repairs.
- Are you confident with a paint can? Do you tend to make cosmetic repairs better or worse?
- Do you have the time to invest in a project? Little and often can work, but some jobs need hours-on-end intensive attention
- What do you want as an end result? A concourse scooter or just something that you can use every day?
- What resources do you have to call on when things go wrong? List friends, workshops, internet forums and mechanical reference books in this category

Don't expect to restore and have something showroom fresh as an end result – if this is what you seek, you should invest more to begin with in your search for a bike and look to buy something that is already running and is proven to be reliable.

There is one overarching question concerning taking on a project that needs answering, and you won't be able to answer it until you go to view the bike. It is, simply, do you feel capable of turning this bike around? Based on your mechanical experience and limits, it should be an easy decision either way just by looking over the bike.

14 What's it worth?
– setting a price

If you have used the marking system in Chapter 11, you'll know where the scooter ranks between perfect to poor condition – most likely somewhere in-between.

You can pick up a printed vehicle price guide from a newsagent, or find a website that has up-to-date values. Enthusiasts' magazines often publish price guides, too. If you haven't bought the latest editions, do so now, or look at classifieds listings online, and compare their suggested values for the model you are thinking of buying; also look at the auction prices they're reporting (refer to Chapter 5 for a guide on where to look). Magazines such as *Parkers* and online sources like *Auto Trader* have reviews and price guides for various models. The values tend to vary from one source to another, as do their scales of condition, so carefully read the guidance notes they provide. Use your assessment of the bike from Chapter 11 to work out the appropriate guide price. How does your assessment compare with the asking price? Before you start haggling with the seller, consider what effect any variation from standard specification might have on the bike's value. If you are buying from a dealer, remember there will be a dealer's premium on the price.

Remember, insurance write-off (Category C or D) bikes may be harder to sell on, so the price you pay if the bike is recorded as damaged/repaired should be lower. Don't expect to fully recoup your purchase price if you sell the bike.

Extras

- Does the bike come with a cover, top box or any other everyday extras?
- In addition to official literature and service history, does the seller have a workshop manual to pass on?
- Bikes that have recently been serviced, and benefit from newer consumable items, such as tyres, will command a greater asking price.
- Prominent within the Vespa model range, limited edition models are rare, and hence more expensive to buy.
- A bike with two original keys is desirable. For newer Piaggio scooters, the main key is used to re-programme the bike's immobiliser if ever it goes wrong, so this is essential.
- Scooters that have had fewer owners are more desirable, so pricier, but easier to sell on.
- If you're looking at a newer bike, is there any remaining manufacturer warranty, or perhaps warranty coverage from a used bike dealer?

15 The Community

– help from other owners

This chapter gives guidance on where to turn to for key Piaggio advice, once this book has run its course and you've made that bike-buying decision. There's a world of help out there, and a whole load of reading to do in other books and online.

Clubs

The author has been involved with the following Piaggio and Vespa-related clubs in the past and is happy to recommend:
- Vespa Club of Great Britain http://www.vespaclubofbritain.co.uk/
- X9 Owners' Club http://www.x9ownersclub.co.uk/site/
- Piaggio Owners' Club http://piaggioownersclub.com/
- Scooter Community UK www.scootercommunity.co.uk
- London Bikers https://londonbikers.com/

Books

- *Caring for your Scooter – How to maintain & service your 49cc to 125cc twist & go scooter (RAC handbook)* by Trevor Fry, published by Veloce Publishing, ISBN 184584095X and 978-1-845840-95-2.
- *Piaggio and Vespa Scooters (with Carburettor Engines) Service and Repair Manual: 1991 to 2009* by Matthew Coombs and Phil Mather, published by Haynes, ISBN 1844258033 and 978-1844258031.
- *Vespa GTS125, 250 & 300ie, GTV250 & 300ie, LX/LXV125 & 150ie, S125/150ie Service and Repair Manual: 2005-2014* by Matthew Coombs and Phil Mather, published by Haynes, ISBN 085733736X and 978-0857337368.
- *Vespa – The Story of a Cult Classic in Pictures* by Gunther Uhlig, published by Veloce Publishing, ISBN 1845847903 and 978-1-845847-90-6.

Magazines

There are no dedicated magazines for modern Piaggio scooters, but it's worth keeping an eye on the following for occasional Piaggio and Vespa new model reviews, also for product reviews of new accessories that you can use with your scooter:
- *Motorcycle News*
- *Scootering*
- *Scooter Geek*
- *Twist&Go*
- *Bike Magazine*
- *Motorcycle Monthly*
- *Visordown.com*

Trusted garages

Take a look on Piaggio's country-specific website to find your nearest service centre. You can search by bike, so to make sure that your nearest garage will be trained and knowledgeable about your model, and then narrow it down further by finding the nearest workshop to you.

Forums

The internet is awash with useful advice for living with and caring for your Piaggio scooter. Forums are especially helpful, as a simple question about your scooter can reach a worldwide platform that will in turn give you real-world advice. The following websites are most popular and thus best to use:

- http://modernvespa.com/forum/
- http://vespa.proboards.com/
- http://www.scootercommunity.co.uk/forums
- http://www.gtsownersclub.co.uk/forum/
- http://vespaownersclub.com/

16 Vital statistics
– vital data when you need it

Bikes for which this book is applicable, with production dates and engine sizes

Model name	Engine size	Production dates
Piaggio B125/Beverly 125	125cc	2002-2010
Piaggio B125/Beverly 300	300cc	2012-2016
Piaggio Beverly ST350	350cc	2012-2016
Piaggio Fly 50	50cc	2005-2016
Piaggio Fly 50 4T	100cc	2006-2016
Piaggio Fly 125	125cc	2005-2016
Piaggio Hexagon	125cc	1994-2000
Piaggio Liberty 50	50cc	1997-2016
Piaggio Liberty 50 4T	50cc	2001-2010
Piaggio Liberty 125	125cc	2000-2016
Piaggio Medley	125cc	2016
Piaggio Medley	150cc	2016
Piaggio NRG	50cc	1994-2016
Piaggio Sfera 50	50cc	1991-1998
Piaggio Sfera 80	80cc	1993-1998
Piaggio Sfera 125	125cc	1996-1998
Piaggio Skipper	125cc	1993-2004
Piaggio Super Hexagon	125cc	2001-2003
Piaggio Typhoon 50	50cc	1993-2016
Piaggio Typhoon 80	80cc	1994-1998
Piaggio Typhoon 125	125cc	1995-2016
Piaggio X7 125	125cc	2008-2009
Piaggio X7 250	250cc	2008-2009
Piaggio X7 Evo 300	300cc	2010
Piaggio X8 125	125cc	2004-2009
Piaggio X8 150	150cc	2006-2008
Piaggio X8 200	200cc	2004-2005
Piaggio X8 250	250cc	2005-2008
Piaggio X8 400	400cc	2006-2008
Piaggio X9 125	125cc	2001-2008

Model name	Engine size	Production dates
Piaggio X9 200	200cc	2002-2004
Piaggio X9 250	250cc	2001-2008
Piaggio X9 500	500cc	2005-2008
Piaggio X10 Exec	350cc	2009-2016
Piaggio X10 Exec	500cc	2009-2016
Piaggio Xevo 125 (Sport)	125cc	2007-2016
Piaggio Xevo 250	250cc	2007-2011
Piaggio Xevo 400	400cc	2007-2011
Piaggio Zip	50cc	1993-2016
Piaggio Zip SP	50cc	1997-2016
Piaggio Zip 4T	50cc	2001-2016
Piaggio Zip 125	125cc	2001-2004
Piaggio Vespa 946	125cc	2013-2016
Piaggio Vespa ET2	50cc	1997-2004
Piaggio Vespa ET4 50	50cc	2001-2004
Piaggio Vespa ET4 125	125cc	1996-2004
Piaggio Vespa GT 125	125cc	2003-2006
Piaggio Vespa GT 200	200cc	2003-2006
Piaggio Vespa GTS 125 (SS, Super, SS ABS, Super ABS, Super IE	125cc	2007-2016
Piaggio Vespa GTS 250 (ie, ABS)	250cc	2005-2012
Piaggio Vespa GTS 300 (SS, Super, SS ABS, Super ABS, Touring)	300cc	2007-2016
Piaggio Vespa GTV 125	125cc	2007-2009
Piaggio Vespa GTV 250	250cc	2007-2009
Piaggio Vespa LX 50 (Touring)	50cc	2005-2013
Piaggio Vespa LX4 125 (Touring)	125cc	2005-2013
Piaggio Vespa LXV 50	50cc	2006-2009
Piaggio Vespa LXV 125	125cc	2006-2009
Piaggio Vespa Primavera 125 (3V, ABS, Touring)	125cc	2014-2016
Piaggio Vespa Primavera 50 (2T, Touring)	50cc	2014-2016
Piaggio Vespa S 50	50cc	2007-2013
Piaggio Vespa S 125 (Sport)	125cc	2007-2013
Piaggio Vespa Sprint 125 (3V, ABS)	125cc	2015-2016

Piaggio family engines

Certain Piaggio engines gain nicknames, usually based on acronyms. Basic information for the engine that is powering your bike is revealed below.

Engine name	Displacement	Valves	Cooling	Cycle	Power
i-get	50cc	3v	Air-cooled	Otto 4T	Varied
i-get	125cc	3v	Air-cooled	Otto 4T	10.9bhp
i-get	150cc	3v	Air-cooled	Otto 4T	13.1bhp
i-get	125cc	4v	Liquid cooled	Otto 4T	12.2bhp
i-get	150cc	4v	Liquid cooled	Otto 4T	15bhp
Hi-PER 2	50cc	N/A	Air-cooled	Otto 2T	Varied
Hi-PER 2	50cc	N/A	Liquid cooled	Otto 2T	Varied
Hi-PER 4	50cc	2v	Air-cooled	Otto 4T	Varied
Hi-PER 4	100cc	2v	Air-cooled	Otto 4T	Varied
Hi-PER 4	50cc	4v	Air-cooled	Otto 4T	Varied
125cc HE	125cc	3v	Air-cooled	Otto 4T	10.1bhp
LEm	125cc	3v	Air-cooled	Otto 4T	11.6bhp
LEm	150cc	3v	Air-cooled	Otto 4T	12.9bhp
LEADER	125cc	2v	Air-cooled	Otto 4T	10.7bhp
LEADER	150cc	2v	Air-cooled	Otto 4T	12.1bhp
MASTER	400cc	4v	Liquid cooled	Otto 4T	34bhp
MASTER	500cc	4v	Liquid cooled	Otto 4T	39.5bhp
Purejet	50cc	N/A	Liquid cooled	Otto 2T	Varied
QUA.S.A.R.	125cc	4v	Liquid cooled	Otto 4T	15bhp
QUA.S.A.R.	250cc	4v	Liquid cooled	Otto 4T	22bhp
QUA.S.A.R.	300cc	4v	Liquid cooled	Otto 4T	22.4bhp
350cc engine	350cc	4v	Liquid cooled	Otto 4T	33.3bhp

The Essential Buyer's Guide™ series ...